Grazing America

Iconic foods from cities across the country

Recipes collected, modified, and occasionaly improved by

Mark Donnelly, PhD.

Text and Design by Mark D. Donnelly, PhD.

RPSS - Rock Paper [Safety] Scissors Publishing
429 Englewood Avenue • Buffalo, New York 14223

www.rpsspublishing.com

ISBN: 978-1-956688-15-3

Printed in the United States of America

19 20 21 22 23 6 5 4 3 2 1

RPSS - ROCK PAPER [SAFETY] SCISSORS PUBLISHING

This book is a road map to the powerful calorie delivery systems that sustain our great cities.

Iconic foods from cities across the country

0 4 6 8 10 12 14 16 18 20 22 24 26 28 30 32 34 36 38 40 42 44 46 48 50
0 50 100 150 200 250 300
CAPACITY 350 LBS.

Dear Flabby,

Coast-to-Coast, we are a nation of local tastes and conspicuous calories. From Rochester, New York's Garbage Plate and Detroit, Michigan's Boogaloo sandwich to Hawaii's Spam Musubi and Biloxi, Mississippi's Koolickles, our regional foods in the United States are deeply embedded into our local culinary consciousness.

These hometown delicacies are a marriage of cultures, subtleties of tradition, local ingredients, and, above all, community. These morsels of scale-tipping pride are equal parts civic symbols, edible tourist attractions, and cultural obsessions.

This book features the birthplace of many of the foods we love. Some seemingly strange combinations are a little hard to get your head around until you take your first bite. Please note: none of them will make you skinny.

These recipes, which I've been collecting for decades from many long-lost sources, are an homage to our immense bounty of our great country's uber-local foods and a great excuse to putter in the kitchen.

New York City, New York:
NY Style Cheesecake

Crust:

2 cups graham cracker crumbs

1/3 cup granulated sugar

1/4 teaspoon ground cinnamon

Pinch of salt

1/2 cup melted butter

Filling:

3 8-ounce packages cream cheese

1 1/2 cups granulated sugar

2 teaspoons vanilla extract

5 eggs

Pinch of salt

5 eggs

1/2 cup sour cream

1/2 cup heavy whipping cream

Topping:

1/2 cup sour cream

2 teaspoons granulated sugar

1/2 teaspoon vanilla extract

Whipped cream for serving

It's much easier to change your self-image than resist eating NY Style cheesecake. On the theory that denial has merit, repeat to yourself–fluffy is good, fluffy is good. Then order- another slice.

Preheat oven to 475°F.
Prepare a 9-inch springform pan with cooking spray. On a flat surface place the pan in the middle of a large 18-inch by 18-inch square of aluminum foil. Fold up the foil's sides around the pan, careful not to create any holes. Fold the top of the foil sheets around the top edge of the pan.

In a medium-size bowl combine the graham cracker crumbs, sugar, cinnamon, and salt. Stir in the melted butter. Use the bottom of a drinking glass to press the crumb mixture into the bottom of the springform pan and about 2/3 the way up the side. Place in the oven for 10 minutes. Remove and let cool. Reduce the oven temperature to 350°F.

Place cream cheese, sugar, vanilla, eggs, and salt in the stand mixer bowl. Beat with the paddle attachment until smooth and creamy. Add the sour cream, lemon zest, and heavy cream and mix until incorporated. Pour into the cooled crust.

Bring a kettle of water to a boil. Place the springform pan in a large, high-sided roasting pan. Pour in enough hot water to come about halfway up the side of the springform pan. Bake for 50 to 60 minutes, or until the top of the cheesecake turns a light brown color. Remove from the oven and roasting pan to cool.

Combine sour cream, vanilla, and sugar. Spread topping over the cheesecake. Chill in the refrigerator for at least 4 hours.
Serve cheesecake with giant mounds of whipped cream.

Avoid mirrors and scales. Fluffy is good.

PIZZERIA
DUE
ELF PARK
Entrance On
Ohio Street
First 30 Minutes $5
ONE
WAY
OHIO ST
PIZZERIA
UNO
Daniel Schwer

Chicago, Illinois:
Deep Dish Pizza

1¾ cups all-purpose flour
¼ cup of yellow cornmeal
¾ teaspoon sea salt
2 teaspoons granulated sugar
1 teaspoon active dry yeast
½ cup warm water
2 tablespoons of unsalted butter, softened to room temperature
2 tablespoons unsalted butter, melted
1½ tablespoons olive oil for coating

Pizza sauce ingredients:

1 tablespoons olive oil, divided
½ tablespoon unsalted butter
¼ of a red onion, minced
½ teaspoon salt
½ teaspoon black pepper
¼ teaspoon Italian seasoning mix
Crushed red pepper flakes to taste
2 cloves garlic, minced
14 ounces crushed tomatoes
½ teaspoon granulated sugar
1 tablespoons fresh basil, chopped

Cont.

Pizza in the United States is deeply embedded into the nation's culinary consciousness, from thin crust in New York to wood fired in San Francisco. But Chicago's version took the concept in a much more indulgent direction, filling a thick crust with inverted layers of cheese, meat and tomatoes, all of it creeping up the side of an oiled steel pan.

It is often reported that Chicago-style deep-dish pizza was invented at Pizzeria Uno in Chicago, in 1943, by Uno's founder Ike Sewell.

Prep the pizza dough:
Combine the flour, cornmeal, sea salt, sugar and active dry yeast in the bowl of a stand mixer fitted with the dough hook attachment. Mix the ingredients together on low.

Stir in the warm water and melted butter, making sure both have cooled enough that they will not kill the yeast. Beat the ingredients together on a low speed until the dough becomes soft and supple. The mixture should start to gently pull away from the sides of the bowl and fall off the dough hook after about 5 minutes of mixing.

Remove the dough from the bowl and roll it into a ball. Place the ball of dough into a lightly greased mixing bowl and rotate the dough until all of its sides are coated in the olive oil. Tightly cover the bowl with tin foil and allow the dough to rise in a warm environment until it doubles in size - about 1 or 2 hours.

After the dough rises, lightly flour a workspace and set the dough on the counter. Gently punch the dough down to get rid of air bubbles before rolling the dough into a large rectangle.

Spread the softened butter on top of the dough, then roll the dough up lengthwise into a log. Cut the log of dough in half and form the 2 pieces of dough into balls. Place the dough back into the large, greased bowl, re-cover it with tin foil and let it rise in the refrigerator for about an hour until the dough is puffy.

Chicago, Illinois: Deep Dish Pizza, cont.

Make the pizza sauce:
As the dough rises, make the pizza sauce by combining 1 tablespoon of olive oil and the butter in a saucepan over medium heat. Mix in the minced onion, Italian seasoning, crushed red pepper, salt, and pepper, and cook until the onion softens. Add the garlic and cook until fragrant. Pour in the tomatoes and sugar, then bring the sauce to a simmer.

Lower the heat and continue stirring for about half an hour until the sauce has reduced. Remove from the heat and sprinkle in the fresh basil and remaining olive oil.

Preheat oven to 475°F
Use a solid metal pan, preferably a deep-sided iron skillet, and melt a thin layer of butter in the pan.

Roll the dough to about 1/3-inch thick and large enough in circumference so it can be placed in the pan with about 1/2 inch hanging over the edges. Place the dough in the pan.

Place your protein ingredients in the bottom of the pan. Top the pan with handfuls of shredded mozzarella cheese. Top with veggies of choice.

Roll out another round layer of dough large enough in circumference to cover the top of the pan. Lay the dough on top like you are topping a pie. Tear 5 or 6 holes in the dough for ventilation. Crimp the edges of the dough around the edges of the pan to create a seal, just like a pie. Trim the edges of the dough at the top of the pan to remove the excess.

Top with a 1/4 inch of your favorite pizza or tomato sauce and a sprinkle of grated Parmesan cheese.

Bake for 25-30 minutes, until the crust is golden brown or the internal temperature is 180°F. Slice, serve, and enjoy!

Toppings:

2 cups mozzarella cheese, shredded

1/4 cup of Parmesan cheese, grated

Additional toppings, such as pepperoni, crumbled sausage, ham, bacon, mushrooms, green peppers, spinach, onions or whatever else you desire

Cincinati, Ohio:
Four-Way Chili

2 pounds ground beef

1 (6-oz) can tomato paste

4 cups water

1 (8-oz) can tomato sauce

1 large onion, minced

6 cloves garlic, minced

3 tablespoons chili powder

1 teaspoon cumin

1 teaspoon cinnamon

¾ teaspoon ground allspice

¼ teaspoon ground cloves

½ teaspoon cayenne

2 teaspoons kosher salt

Outside of Cincinnati, Cincinnati-style chili is known as "that weird cinnamon chili on spaghetti." But around Cincinnati, it's a way of life. And they serve it their way:

2-Way: Chili served over spaghetti.
3-Way: Chili served over spaghetti with finely shredded cheddar cheese.
4-Way: Chili served over spaghetti with diced onions and finely shredded cheddar cheese.
5-Way: Chili served over spaghetti with warmed canned red kidney beans, diced onions, and finely shredded cheddar cheese.

Heat a large, heavy-bottomed pot or Dutch oven over medium-high heat. Add the tomato paste to the dry pot and cook, constantly scraping the bottom until the tomato smells rich and toasty and you start to see browned (not burned) patches in the bottom of the pot. This should take 1 to 3 minutes.

Combine the ingredients in a pot. Remove the pot from heat and add the ground beef and water. Mix them together into a sludge. Return to medium-high heat and bring to a simmer, stirring all the while, so the sludge breaks up into a mealy paste. Add all the remaining ingredients except the vinegar and chocolate.

Simmer gently, uncovered, for 2 to 3 hours, stirring often. Add the vinegar and chocolate.

Serve any "way".

Wildwood, New Jersey: Jersey Breakfast Dogs

This Garden State breakfast adventure is a morning adaptation of "the Ripper." It's listed as number two on Esquire Magazine's *"60 Things Worth Shortening Your Life For."*

In a corkscrew fashion, wrap each hot dog with one slice of bacon, using toothpicks as needed to hold the bacon in place.

Pour oil into a deep fryer or heavy-bottom pot and fry the wrapped hot dog at 375°F until cooked and the bacon is crispy.

Transfer to a plate lined with a paper towel to drain. Unless you have a death wish, remove the toothpicks before eating.

In a medium skillet, cook the additional bacon until crispy. Remove from the skillet and set aside, reserving the grease.

Fry onions in the bacon grease until lightly browned. Add the chili and heat through.

Put deep-fried, bacon-wrapped hot dog on bun, and top with chili, onions, bacon, and cheese.

Top with a fried egg because, after all, this is for breakfast.

6 quarter-pound beef hot dogs

12 slices bacon

6 hot dog buns

1 cup chili

1 medium onion, chopped

1 cup sharp cheddar cheese, shredded

6 fried eggs

Oil for deep frying

O‘ahu, Hawaii: Spam Musubi

2 slices Spam cut in ⅜ inch slices

1 teaspoon butter

3 ounces cooked white rice, seasoned with furikake and toasted sesame seeds, if desired

1 whole sheet nori

1 tablespoon sweet ginger-sesame sauce

Recipe Source: SPAM website

Spam musubi originally came to Hawaii from Japan. It is popular item among the lunchboxes of Hawaiian plantation workers.

The origin of Spam musubi is disputed. Survivors of the Japanese American internment camps on the mainland of the United States claim to have invented the precursor to Spam musubi when they placed seasoned slices of Spam on white rice in a baking pan. However, most origin stories focus on Spam's ubiquity in Hawaii during and after World War II. With few other options, the canned meat was incorporated into local cuisines wherever American troops were stationed.

In a large skillet, fry Spam in butter until lightly browned and crisp. Place half of the rice into a musubi press or small can. Place Spam Classic on rice; drizzle with ginger-sesame sauce. Top with remaining rice; press down.

Remove Spam and rice from musubi press. On work surface, lay nori shiny-side-down; top with Spam mixture. Wrap up. Cut each musubi in half. Slice each half diagonally into 2 pieces. Serve immediately.

If this Spam experience proves positive, be sure to try "Lobster Thermidor aux crevettes with a Mornay sauce, served in a Provençale manner with shallots and aubergines, garnished with truffle pâté, brandy, a fried egg on top, and Spam."

"Spam, lovely Spam, wonderful Spam."
-Monty Python's Flying Circus

2445-NR
MI 3000
K62-FHV
H15-521H

Buffalo, New York: Chicken Wings

Oil for frying

5 pounds chicken wings

8 tablespoon (1 stick) butter

5 tablespoons Frank's hot sauce

Celery sticks

Blue cheese dressing

"Wings," or chicken wings, are the perfect blue-collar dish from a blue-collar town. Locals cringe while traveling and seeing "Buffalo wings" on a menu. As a city, Buffalonians all know that Buffalos are flightless hairy mammals that smell when wet. The only charitable explanation is that the "Buffalo" designation is driving directions to the city where you can get the real thing.

Legend has it their invention came about at The Anchor Bar in Buffalo because of a mistake—the delivery of some chicken wings instead of the backs and necks that were ordnarily used in making spaghetti sauce. Upon the unannounced, late-night arrival the owner's son, with several of his friends from college, they came up with the idea of deep frying chicken wings (normally thrown away or reserved for stock) and tossing them in cayenne hot sauce.

In a heavy-bottomed Dutch oven or electric deep fryer, heat oil to 375°F.

Prepare the wings by cutting them into three sections and discarding the tip. Pat them dry.

In a medium sauce pot set over low heat, melt butter and add hot sauce and stir until fully incorporated.

Fry wings in small batches until crispy on the outside and no longer pink on the inside. Drain on paper towels. Transfer wings to a large bowl containing sauce and carefully toss to coat.

Serve with celery sticks and blue cheese dressing
... and an old-growth forest worth of napkins.

Minneapolis, Minnesota:
The Juicy Lucy/Jucy Lucy

A Juicy Lucy or Jucy Lucy is a stuffed burger with cheese inside the meat instead of on top, resulting in a melted core of cheese. Two bars in Minneapolis, Matt's Bar, and the 5-8 Club, furociously claim to be the inventor of this burger. Shirts worn by staff at the 5-8 Club say, "if it's spelled right, it's done right," while advertising for Matt's Bar says, "Remember, if it is spelled correctly, you are eating a shameless rip-off!"

1 ½ pounds ground beef

1 tablespoon Worcestershire sauce

½ teaspoon garlic salt

1 teaspoon black pepper

4 slices American cheese

4 hamburger buns, split

In a large bowl, combine ground beef, Worcestershire sauce, garlic salt, and pepper. Mix well. Form 8, thin patties from the beef. Each patty should be slightly larger than a slice of cheese.

Cut each slice of American cheese into 4 equal pieces; stack the pieces. Sandwich one stack of cheese between 2 ground beef patties. Tightly pinch edges together tightly seal the cheese within the meat.

Preheat a cast-iron or other heavy-bottomed skillet over medium heat. Cook burgers until browned on the outside and no longer pink on the inside; about 4 minutes.

Serve on hamburger buns.

St. Louis, Missouri:
Gooey Butter Cake

1 (18¼ oz) package yellow cake mix
2 eggs
½ cup butter melted
1 (8 oz) package softened cream cheese
2 eggs beaten
1 teaspoon vanilla
3½ cups powdered sugar
Powdered sugar to sprinkle

The cake was supposedly first made by accident in the 1930s by a St. Louis-area German American baker trying to make regular cake batter but accidentally reversed the proportions of butter and flour.

The St. Louis Convention & Visitors Commission includes a recipe on its website, calling it "one of St. Louis' popular, quirky foods". Outside of the St. Louis area, this irresistible combination of sweet and buttery decadence is commonly known as "ooey gooey butter cake".

Preheat oven to 350°F.

In a medium bowl, combine cake mix, 1 egg and butter and mix until smooth. Press into the bottom of a lightly greased 13 by 9-inch baking pan.

Blend cream cheese, 2 eggs, vanilla and powdered sugar until creamy and smooth. Spread over your the first mixture in your pan.

Bake at 350°F for 40-45 minutes or until edges are golden brown. Do not over bake as the center should be a little gooey.

Sprinkle with powdered sugar.

Tampa, Florida:
Cuban Sandwiches

A Cuban sandwich or Cubano is a variation of a ham and cheese sandwich that likely originated around the late 1800s in cafes catering to Cuban workers in Tampa and Key West. By the 1960s, Cuban sandwiches were also common on Miami restaurant menus. The Cuban sandwich was designated the "signature sandwich of the city of Tampa" by the Tampa City Council in 2012

In a large zip-lock bag, place the olive oil, orange juice, lime juice, garlic, oregano, cumin, salt and pepper in a bowl and shake to combine. Place the pork in the bag and refrigerate overnight.

Preheat a grill to medium-high heat and cook for the pork for 8-10 minutes per side or until a meat thermometer registers 145°F. Allow the pork rest before thinly slicing the meat.

Cut the loaf of bread in half lengthwise and then crosswise into 4 equal sized pieces.

Place half of the cheese slices on the bottom pieces of bread. Top with layers of ham, pork and pickles.Add the rest of the cheese on top of the pickles. Spread the mustard over the top pieces of bread, then place the tops on each sandwich.

Coat the outsides of the bread and grill in a panini press until bread is golden brown and cheese is melted.

Cut the sandwiches in half and serve.

¼ cup olive oil
¼ cup orange juice
2 tablespoons lime juice
1 teaspoon minced garlic
½ teaspoon dried oregano
¼ teaspoon ground cumin
Salt and pepper to taste
1 pound pork tenderloin
1 loaf French Bread sliced lengthwise
1 pound Swiss cheese sliced
1 pound smoked ham thinly sliced
4 large dill pickles, thinly sliced crosswise
1 cup yellow mustard
1 tablespoon butter

Philadelphia, Pennsylvania
Philly Cheese Steak

In Philadelphia, the cheesesteak stands as equal parts civic symbol, tourist attraction, and cultural obsession. And no place represents the true grit of this working-class town and speaks to the soul of the city better than the corner of 9th Street and Passyunk Avenue in South Philly, the cheesesteak epicenter. Pat's King of Steaks and Geno's Steaks face off, located close to the Italian Market caddy-corner from each other 24 hours a day.

Philadelphians Pat and Harry Olivieri are often credited with inventing the sandwich by serving chopped steak on an Italian roll in the early 1930s. The exact story behind its creation is foggy at best. Still, in some accounts, Pat and Harry Olivieri originally owned a hot dog stand and, on one occasion, decided to make a new sandwich using chopped beef and grilled onions. While Pat was eating the sandwich, a cab driver stopped by and was interested in it, so he requested one for himself. After eating it, the cab driver suggested that Olivieri quit making hot dogs and instead focus on the new sandwich.

They began selling this variation of steak sandwiches at their hot dog stand near South Philadelphia's Italian Market. They became so popular that Pat opened his restaurant, which still operates today as Pat's King of Steaks. It wasn't until World War II, however, that the cheesesteak became a Philly trademark. As an audacious public relations stunt, Pat began a rumor that his sandwiches contained horse meat because of WWII rationing. Then, in faux outrage, he offered a $10,000 reward for anyone to prove it. Business boomed, and at last count, as many as 96 local competitors followed.

Geno's is the other half of this corner's famous Philly cheesesteak rivalry. Joey Vento founded Geno's in 1966 with only two boxes of steaks, a few hot dogs, and $2,000 from his father-in-law, who was a bookie. Joey's unique selling proposition is that he slices the steak where Pat's chops theirs.

The building Geno's is in was actually condemned at the time. It was originally spelled Gino's, but Gino Marchetti, the football player, already ran Gino's hamburger stand, so they convinced him to change the name to Geno's.

Traditionally, the meat is thinly sliced rib-eye or top round, served on Amoroso hoagie rolls. One source writes, "A proper cheesesteak consists of provolone or Cheez Whiz slathered on an Amoroso roll and stuffed with thinly shaved grilled meat. Cheez Whiz, (just "Whiz" in local parlance), first marketed in 1952, was not yet available for the original 1930 version but has rapidly spread in popularity.

Philly Cheese Steak, Cont.

The Battle of Passyunk Avenue

Pat's King of Steaks Cheesesteak

1 sweet onion, sliced into half rings
½ pound sliced fresh mushrooms, optional
½ green bell pepper, sliced into long strips
6 tablespoons canola oil, divided
¼ cup Cheez Whiz, warmed
1-½ pounds beef ribeye steaks - chopped
4 Amoroso hoagie rolls or crusty Italian rolls, split

In a large skillet, saute the onion and, if desired, mushrooms and peppers in 3 tablespoons oil until tender. Remove and keep warm.

While the onions are cooking, warm the cheese sauce in a small saucepan over low heat.

In the same pan, saute beef in remaining oil in batches. Leave the meat on the grill until the sides start to sizzle and curl up.

On each roll bottom, layer the beef, onion mixture. Drizzle Cheez Whiz. Replace tops.

Geno's Cheesesteak

1 sweet onion, sliced into half rings
½ pound sliced fresh mushrooms, optional
½ green bell pepper, sliced into long strips
6 tablespoons canola oil, divided
¼ cup Cheez Whiz, warmed
1-½ pounds beef ribeye steaks - thinly sliced
4 Amoroso hoagie rolls or crusty Italian rolls, split

In a large skillet, saute the onion and, if desired, mushrooms and peppers in 3 tablespoons oil until tender. Remove and keep warm.

While the onions are cooking, warm the cheese sauce in a small saucepan over low heat.

In the same pan, saute beef in remaining oil in batches. Leave the meat on the grill until the sides start to sizzle and curl up.

On each roll bottom, layer the beef, onion mixture. Drizzle Cheez Whiz. Replace tops.

BONNY

Boston: Massachusetts: Brown Bread

Cooking spray
¾ cup whole wheat flour
¾ cup rye flour
¾ cup cornmeal
1 teaspoon Baking Powder
1 teaspoon. Baking Soda
¾ teaspoon salt
1¼ cups buttermilk
½ cup Blackstrap molasses
6 oz. dark roast coffee, room temperature
¾ cup raisins

Boston brown bread is dark, slightly sweet steamed bread, usually sweetened with molasses, traditionally served with baked beans and franks.

Brown bread started making an appearance in the early 1800s. Early settlers were trying to grow wheat, which was their preferred grain for baking. They soon realized that wheat did not grow well in the New England soil, and this drove up the prices. Corn, on the other hand, was a crop that flourished on the east coast, making the price of cornmeal much cheaper and readily available. Another cheap alternative to flour was rye flour.

These two grains made up the main dry ingredients for the bread. Occasionally whole wheat flour was added and eventually became a mainstay on the ingredient list. Molasses is added, giving the bread its signature rich color and sweet flavor. The batter is traditionally poured into a coffee can and steamed in a kettle. This version uses a normal loaf pan.

Preheat oven to 325°F. Spray an 8½ x 4½-inch loaf pan with cooking spray and set aside.

In a large bowl, sift together wheat flour, rye flour, cornmeal, baking soda, baking powder, and salt. Stir in the buttermilk and molasses, and coffee, mixing just until combined (do not over-mix). Fold in raisins.

Transfer batter to prepared pan, and cover it with buttered (or sprayed) aluminum foil, pressing the foil tight around the edges of the pan (so that the bread will steam a bit), but ballooning it in the center so that the bread has room to expand without hitting the foil. Bake for 50 minutes.

Remove the foil (the middle may be slightly sunken; that's OK), and bake for an additional 10 minutes, or until a toothpick inserted in the center comes out clean.

Detroit Michigan: Boogaloo

Jean's Sauce of the Islands

(The lady that owned Brothers unfortunately took the recipe to the grave. This is recipe is very close.)

2 tablespoons olive oil
1 cup minced onion
2 cloves garlic, minced
2 tablespoons Worcestershire sauce
¾ teaspoon dried thyme
¾ teaspoon dried mustard
2 cups ketchup
½ cup brown sugar
¼ cup black strap molasses
½ cup spiced rum, divided
3 tablespoons hoisin sauce
2 tablespoons tomato paste
2 tablespoons sherry vinegar
1 tablespoon chili powder
¼ teaspoon cayenne pepper

Sandwiches:

1 tablespoon olive oil
1¼ pounds ground pork
1 onion, sliced thin
1 green pepper, chopped
¾ teaspoon pepper
¾ teaspoon salt
1 loaf French bread cut into 6 inch pieces slices lengthwise

On the surface, this may look like a loose burger, a barbecue sandwich, a hoagie, or merely a Detroit-style sloppy Joe. Your first bite will tell you you're off by a Michigan mile. The Boogaloo is bolder and slightly more sophisticated than its loose and sloppy cousins.

In the late '60s, Brothers Bar-B-Que co-owner Jean Johnson invented the sandwich in her well-loved barbecue spot. Originally, Johnson assembled the sandwich with ground pork (it's now typically made with beef), sautéed peppers and onions, and melted American cheese on a grilled, eight-inch sub bun. But what sets it apart is Jean's Sauce of The Islands, a sweet and tangy tomato-based sauce with a distinct Jamaican kick.

For the sauce:
Mix all ingredients together in a small saucepan over medium-high heat. Bring mixture to a boil, reduce to simmer, and cook stirring constantly until slightly thickened; set aside.

For the sandwich:
Preheat oven to 350°F.
Heat oil in 12-inch nonstick skillet over medium-high heat until just smoking. Add pork, onion, green pepper, salt and pepper and cook, until the meat begins to sizzle, about 10 minutes. Add 1 cup sauce and bring to boil. Reduce heat to medium and simmer about 1 minute until slightly thickened.

Place rolls on a baking sheet and divide meat mixture evenly among roll bottoms. Top each sandwich with 2 slices American cheese. Bake until cheese is melted and rolls are warmed through, about 5 minutes. Divide remaining sauce equally among sandwiches. Fold roll tops over meat and serve.

Harlem, New York: Chicken & Waffles

Chicken and Waffles first appeared in the United States in the 1600s in Pennsylvania Dutch country. They consisted of a plain waffle with pulled, stewed chicken on top, covered in gravy.

A soul food version using fried chicken served as it would be for breakfast, with condiments such as butter and syrup first appeared with the opening of the Wells Supper Club in Harlem, New York, in 1938.

Since the 1970s, chicken and waffles have regained popularity in Los Angeles due to the fame of Roscoe's House of Chicken and Waffles.

Preheat your waffle iron.
In a medium-sized bowl, whisk together the flour, sugar, baking powder, and salt.

Add the melted butter, eggs, and vanilla extract in a small bowl and whisk well to combine. Add the wet ingredients to the dry ingredients and stir to combine. Add waffle mix to your hot waffle iron and cook according to your waffle iron's instructions.

In a large bowl, stir together buttermilk, salt, garlic powder, onion powder, white pepper, and smoked paprika. Add in chicken tenderloins. Be sure all chicken pieces are saturated in the mixture.

Cover the bowl and let the chicken marinate in the mixture in the fridge overnight. In a large cast iron/dutch oven, heat oil to 350°F.

In a shallow pie plate, whisk together flour and seasonings. Take each chicken piece and shake off the excess buttermilk mixture, then dip it into seasoned flour and coat chicken all over.

Fry chicken in small batches until golden brown and crispy, about 7-10 minutes, or until cooked through completely.

Place two pieces of chicken on a waffle and serve with butter and maple syrup.

Buttermilk Waffles:

2 cups all purpose flour
¼ cup sugar
4 teaspoons baking powder
½ teaspoon salt
¼ cup butter, melted
2 cups milk
2 large eggs
2 teaspoons vanilla extract

Fried Chicken:

1 lb chicken tenderloins
1 cup whole buttermilk
1 teaspoon kosher salt
1 teaspoon garlic powder
1 teaspoon onion powder
½ teaspoon white pepper
½ teaspoon smoked paprika
Vegetable oil, about 1.5 quarts for frying

Springfield, Illinois: The Horseshoe Sandwich

3 cups French-fried potatoes

Beer Cheese Sauce:

2 tablespoons butter

2 tablespoons all-purpose flour

¼ teaspoon salt

⅛ teaspoon ground mustard

⅛ teaspoon pepper

¾ cup milk

1 cup white cheddar cheese, shredded

¼ cup beer, room temperature

¾ teaspoon Worcestershire sauce

1 boneless ham steak, cooked, cut into quarters

4 slices Texas toast, toasted

Paprika

The horseshoe sandwich was invented in Springfield, Illinois, in 1928 by Leland Hotel chef Joe Schweska. The Leland fell on hard times and closed in October 1970. It's said that the only enduring legacy is the horseshoe, with five horseshoes being their last meals served, even as the electricity was being cut off.

While hamburger has now become the most common meat on a horseshoe, the original meat was ham. The "horseshoe" name has been attributed to the horseshoe-like shape of a slice of bone-in ham. The sandwich and fries are covered with a "beer cheese" Welsh rarebit-style mixture which is curious since prohibition didn't end until 1929.

Cook potatoes according to package directions.

In a small saucepan over medium heat, melt butter. Stir in flour, salt, mustard, and pepper until smooth; gradually whisk in milk. Bring to a boil, stirring constantly until thickened.

Reduce heat and stir in cheese until blended. Add beer and Worcestershire sauce and heat through.

In a large skillet over medium-high heat, cook ham until heated through and lightly browned.

To serve, toast on each plate, top with ham, fries, and beer cheese sauce. Lightly sprinkle with paprika.

Utica, New York:
Utica Greens

Utica greens is a signature Italian American dish popularized by Joe Morelle in the late 1980s at the Chesterfield Restaurant in Utica, N.Y., where it is on his menu as greens Morelle. Many of the Italian restaurants in Utica began serving this variation on traditional Sicilian and Southern Italian sauteed greens as a side dish or an appetizer.

There is even an annual Utica Greens Fest in Utica every fall, which features lots of food and art.

- 1 head escarole, chopped and rinsed
- 3 tablespoons olive oil
- ½ cup prosciutto, diced
- ½ onion, chopped
- 3 cloves garlic, minced
- 5 hot pickled cherry peppers, chopped
- ½ cup chicken stock
- Salt and pepper to taste
- ½ cup bread crumbs
- ¼ cup parmesan cheese grated

In a large stock pot filled with enough salted water to cover greens, boil and blanch until tender. Drain in a colander and run under cold water.

In a frying pan, heat the olive oil. Add the prosciutto and onion and cook for about 5 minutes.

Add the garlic and cook for another minute.

Add the drained escarole, cherry peppers, and chicken stock and stir together. Cook until the escarole is wilted, about 7-8 minutes.

Sprinkle the top with bread crumbs and cheese, and stick under the broiler for 2 minutes to brown the top.

New Jersey:
Disco Fries

2 lbs. of steak-cut or crinkle-cut french fries

8 oz. mozzarella cheese, shredded

3 cups beef or chicken gravy

2 teaspoons Worcestershire sauce

Salt and pepper to taste

These steak-cut french fries bathed in gravy and gooey mozzarella cheese called Disco Fries is a New Jersey diner classic. It's said that they're called that because they were the preferred late-night meal of the polyester-clad disco crowd at its peak from the mid-'70s to early '80s. Disco Fries are kind of like the Jersey version of Canada's Poutine.

Preheat the oven to 425°F.

Spread the fries in one single layer on a large baking sheet. Cook the fries until golden and crispy.

While the fries are cooking, heat the gravy. Add in the Worcestershire and season to taste with salt and pepper. Remove from heat.

When the fries are done, evenly sprinkle with the shredded mozzarella cheese. Return to the oven 2-3 minutes until the cheese is melted. Pour the warm gravy on top and garnish.

Get up and boogie. Enjoy!

New Haven, Connecticut: White Clam Pizza

1- Ready-made pizza dough ball for 16" pie

Topping:

¾ cup chopped fresh clams

¼ cup olive oil, plus more for drizzling

1 teaspoon dried oregano

4 cloves garlic, minced

¾ cup shredded mozzarella, optional

½ cup grated Parmesan

Kosher salt to taste

1 tablespoon chopped parsley

Crushed red pepper, for serving

Evidence shows that the Wampanoag tribe of present-day Southern New England and Cape Cod ate pies made from clams before encountering English Settlers in the early 1600s. Pies had been common in medieval Europe, and the English settlers to the Plymouth Colony cooked a variety of pies because it was a sure way to preserve foods, so it kept meats and seafood fresh through the long winters before refrigeration.

A clam pie is a savory pie prepared using clams as a main ingredient. Ingredients in addition to whole or chopped clams and pie crust can include potatoes, corn, onion, celery, garlic, clam juice, milk, eggs, hard-boiled eggs, butter, crushed crackers, seasonings, salt and pepper.

Place the dough in a warm area until it doubles in size, about 2 hours.

For the topping:
Mostly drain the clams, retaining about 2 tablespoons liquid. Mix the chopped clams, juice, olive oil, oregano, and garlic in a bowl. Keep refrigerated until ready to use.

Preheat the oven to 500°F and adjust the rack to the lowest level.

Turn the dough onto a lightly floured baking sheet and stretch it into a very thin 16-inch circle. Sprinkle the dough with mozzarella, top evenly with the clam mixture and Parmesan cheese, and season with salt.

Cook until golden brown on top and bottom, 8 -10 minutes. Sprinkle with parsley and crushed red pepper. Drizzle with more olive oil.

How Cities Put on the Dog

When it comes to eating tube steaks, people in different cities get it on in different ways.

New York City
Typically sold from the sidewalk cart, hot dogs in the Big Apple are adorned with little more than brown mustard and onions stewed in tomato paste.

Kansas City
Dorothy clicks her ruby heels to go home to a fusion of the traditional ballpark frank and the Reuben sandwich. All stacked high with corned beef and Swiss; these all-beef dogs are typically topped with melted cheese, caraway, sauerkraut, and Thousand Island dressing.

New Jersey
New Jersey is known for its deep-fried hot dogs that burst open, splitting their outer casing. Affectionately called "Rippers," these heart attacks on a bun are often served with mustard, relish, onions, carrots and cabbage.

Atlanta
Atlantans love to order their savory dogs blanketed with coleslaw or "dragged through the garden."

Chicago
Iconic dogs from the Windy City come buried with an array of toppings, including fresh tomatoes, pickle spears, hot peppers, relish, and onion. Don't even think about requesting ketchup.

Montréal
Whether you get steamed "steamies," or griddle fried "toasties," the hockey players and other residents of Montréal like their dogs topped with coleslaw, onion, mustard, relish, and occasionally paprika or chili powder.

Buffalo
Long before Buffalo invented its famous wings, the legendary Ted's Hot Dogs was charcoal broiling over real hardwood. Available in both a regular, foot-long size, they come dressed with ketchup, mustard, onion, relish, and a special hot sauce.

Memphis, Tennessee: Grilled PBJB&B

3 slices bacon

2 slices Hawaiian bread

1 tablespoon peanut butter

½ banana, sliced

1 teaspoon honey

Bacon grease for grilling

Before you bust your next Elvis move, be sure to eat a Cadillac-load of the King's favorite food: a grilled peanut butter and banana sandwich with bacon.

Jiggling your girth in a silver lamé jumpsuit has much more flair after chowing down on what CNN referred to as a "gooey concoction, fatter than a herd of hogs."

In a small, cast iron pan, cook bacon until extra crispy. Leave the bacon grease in pan for grilling the sandwich.

On one slice of bread, spread a thick layer of peanut butter. Place banana slices on top.

On the other slice of bread, spread a layer of honey. Place 3 bacon slices on top.

Combine the two halves and grill in the bacon grease at medium heat until golden brown and crispy.

Cut the sandwich diagonally with wildly gyrating pelvic thrusts.

Serve warm.

Biloxi, Mississippi: Koolickles

This seemingly strange combination is a little hard to get your head around until you take your first bite. These sweet and sour gherkins, which are actually a pretty mainstream treat in some parts of the South. They're great fun at a party and a runaway hit with kids and pregnant women.

Drain the juice from the jar of pickles into an empty gallon container.

Add the Kool-Aid and sugar to the pickle juice and mix until the sugar is completely dissolved.

Pour the now modified juice back into the jar of pickles, making sure that the pickles are completely covered. Refrigerate.

Your Koolickles will be ready to delight and amaze in approximately one week.

6 large Kosher Dill pickles

1 package cherry Kool-Aid, unsweetened

1 cup granulated sugar

Lancaster, Pennsylvania: Whoopie Pies

Whoopie pies originated in Lancaster County and are one of Pennsylvania Dutch Country's best-known and most-loved comfort foods for locals and visitors alike.

They were created by Lancaster's Amish and Pennsylvania German communities and have been handed down for years in home kitchens and small bakeries from generation to generation. It's believed that whoopie pies were first made from leftover cake batter. Amish legend has it that when children and even farmers would find the delicious treat in their lunch pail, they'd yell out, "Whoopie!"

Preheat oven to 400°F.

In a large bowl, add the cake mix, water, and dry pudding mix. Beat until smooth.

Create 4-inch circles of batter on a lightly greased baking pan using a small ice-cream scoop. Bake for 10 to 12 minutes. Remove from the pan and place on a rack to cool. Repeat until all of the batter is used.

In a medium-sized bowl, beat together the butter, sugar, Marshmallow Fluff, and vanilla until well blended.

Spread 2 tablespoons of filling onto half of the cookies. Sandwich together with remaining half.

Whoopie pies are best eaten in the back seat of a horse-drawn carriage.

1 Devil's food cake mix

1 cup water

1 package (3 oz.) instant chocolate pudding

Filling:

8 tablespoons butter (1 stick)

1½ cups confectioners' sugar

2 cups Marshmallow Fluff

1½ teaspoons pure vanilla extract

Key West, Florida: Key Lime Pie

Graham Cracker Crust:

1 ½ cups graham cracker crumbs
⅓ cup granulated sugar
6 tablespoons butter melted

Key Lime Filling:

28 oz. sweetened condensed milk
½ cup light sour cream
¾ cup Key lime juice
Zest from 2 regular limes
or 4 key limes

Whipped Cream Topping:

1 cup heavy whipping cream
½ cup powdered sugar
1 teaspoon vanilla extract

Key lime pie is probably derived from the "Magic Lemon Cream Pie" published in a promotional brochure by Borden, a producer of condensed milk, in 1931. The recipe is attributed to Borden's fictional spokesperson, Jane Ellison, and includes condensed milk, lemon juice and rind, and egg yolks. It is covered with meringue, baked, and served cold. According to the pastry chef Stella Parks, users of the recipe altered it with local ingredients. It was in the 1950s that Key lime pie was promoted as Florida's "most famous treat" and in 1987 as "the greatest of all regional American desserts."

Graham cracker crust:
Preheat oven to 375°F.
Mix graham cracker crumbs, sugar, and butter in a small bowl. Press the crumb mixture into an 8" - 9.5" pie pan. Bake for 7 minutes. Cool for at least 30 minutes.

Key Lime Filling:
Preheat oven to 350°F.

Whisk together sweetened condensed milk, sour cream, lime juice, and lime zest in a medium bowl. Pour into prepared graham cracker crust and bake for 10 minutes.

Let the pie cool slightly before chilling. Chill for at least 3 hours.

Whipped Cream Topping:
Beat heavy cream and sugar together in a mixer until stiff peaks form. Beat in vanilla. Spread or pipe the whipped cream on top of the cooled pie. Top with additional lime zest if desired.

Rhode Island:
Coffee Milk

While the precise origin of coffee milk is unclear, several sources trace it back to the 19th-century Italian immigrant population in Providence, Rhode Island. In the late 19th and early 20th centuries, approximately 55,000 Italian immigrants traveled to Providence, introducing their traditions and customs to Rhode Island; this included drinking sweetened coffee with milk, which is believed to have led to the creation of coffee milk.

Coffee milk originated in American diners and soda fountains in the early 20th century. The first coffee syrup is thought to have been created by a soda fountain operator who sweetened leftover coffee grounds with milk and sugar to create a syrup, then mixed it into glasses of milk. In the 1930s, coffee milk was regularly served at pharmacy lunch counters, targeted toward children as an alternative to the hot coffee served to their parents.

In 1993, the Rhode Island General Assembly officially named Coffee milk the state drink.

½ cup finely ground coffee

2 cups cold water

1 cup sugar

Each Serving:

1 cup cold milk

Brew a cup of coffee.

In a small saucepan, combine coffee and sugar; bring to a boil. Reduce heat; simmer until reduced by half, about 30 minutes. Remove from heat; transfer to a small bowl or covered container. Refrigerate, covered, until cold or up to 2 weeks.

To prepare coffee milk: In a tall glass, mix 1 cup milk and 2-4 tablespoons coffee milk syrup.

Nashville, Tennessee: Hot Chicken

The first bite of a Nashville Hot Chicken sandwich should send your taste buds screaming, walking the thin line between pleasure and pain. It's savory, salty, spicy, hot, and totally addicting.

Legend has it, this fiery spice blend is the work of a scorned Nashville woman whose fried chicken-loving partner, Thornton Prince, had a habit of coming home late with a little more than sweat around his collar. After a particularly debaucherous night, Prince woke up to the smell of freshly cooked fried chicken. Little did he know, his partner had put a devilish amount of cayenne pepper in his dish to teach him a lesson. Her plan backfired, however, because he ended up loving it so much that he took her recipe and opened the first Nashville Hot Chicken shop.

Toss chicken with black pepper, cayenne pepper, paprika and 2 tablespoons salt in a large bowl. Cover and chill at least 3 hours. Whisk eggs, buttermilk, and hot sauce in a large bowl. Mix flour and remaining tablespoon salt in another large bowl.

Add 2" oil to the Dutch oven and heat over medium-high heat until the thermometer registers 325F°.

Pat chicken dry. Dredge each piece of chicken in flour mixture, shaking off excess, then dip in buttermilk mixture. Dredge again in flour mixture.

Fry chicken in batches, turning occasionally, until skin is crisp and golden brown (15–18 minutes).
Mix cayenne, brown sugar, chili powder, garlic powder, onion powder, paprika, salt, and pepper in a medium bowl; carefully whisk in ½ cup frying oil and ¼ cup melted butter.

Brush fried chicken with spicy oil. Serve with bread and pickles.

10 boneless, skinless chicken thighs
1 tablespoon cayenne pepper
1 tablespoon black pepper
1 teaspoon paprika
3 tablespoons kosher salt
4 large eggs
2 cups buttermilk
1/4 cup Frank's hot sauce
4 cups all-purpose flour
10 cups vegetable oil for frying
4 tablespoons cayenne pepper
2 tablespoons brown sugar
1 teaspoon chili powder blend
1 teaspoon garlic powder
1 teaspoon onion powder
1 teaspoon paprika
1 ½ teaspoons kosher salt
1 teaspoon black pepper
½ cup used frying oil
¼ cup butter
10 hamburger buns
Dill pickle slices

Mackinac Island, Michigan: Pasty

- 3 cups all-purpose flour, plus extra for rolling dough
- 1 cup shortening
- Kosher salt
- 1 cup water - ice cold
- 8 oz. ground beef
- 4 ounces rutabaga, cut into ¼-inch dice
- 1 medium carrot, cut into ¼-inch dice
- 1 small yellow onion, finely chopped
- 1 small russet potato, peeled and cut into ¼-inch dice
- ¼ cup picked fresh parsley leaves, chopped
- Freshly ground black pepper
- 1 egg, whisked
- Ketchup, for serving

When Cornish miners migrated to Michigan's Upper Peninsula in the 1800s, they brought their beloved national dish: the Pasty. The Finnish miners that followed adopted these meat pies as their own because they were easily transportable for long subterranean days.

Pasties are a significant tourist attraction in some areas of the Upper Peninsula of Michigan, including an annual Pasty Fest in Calumet, Michigan, in mid-August.

Preheat the oven to 350F°. Line a baking sheet with parchment paper.

Add the flour, shortening, and a pinch of salt to a food processor and run until the dough clumps together. With the motor running, drizzle in the water until a ball forms. Wrap the dough in plastic and refrigerate for about 1 hour.

Mix together the beef, rutabaga, carrots, onions, potatoes and parsley. Sprinkle with salt and pepper.

Cut the cold dough into 6 even pieces and form into balls. Flour a work surface and roll out each ball of dough into an 8-inch circle. Evenly divide the filling (about 3/4 cup per Pasty) on half of each dough circle. Fold the dough to cover the mixture and crimp the edges using a fork. Slice 3 small slits on top of each pocket. Brush the pasties with the egg and bake on the prepared baking sheet until the crust is golden brown and flaky (about 1 hour 15 minutes).

Serve with ketchup.

Louisville, Kentucky: Hot Browns

½ cup butter

½ cup all-purpose flour

3 cups milk

2 cups shredded sharp white cheddar cheese (6 ounces)

1 egg, beaten

2 tablespoons heavy cream

Few dashes of hot sauce

8 slices white bread, toasted

2 pounds sliced roasted turkey

1 tomato, thinly sliced

Salt and pepper to taste

¼ cup freshly grated Parmigiano-Reggiano cheese

16 strips crispy bacon

A Hot Brown is an open-faced hot turkey sandwich created at the Brown Hotel in Louisville, Kentucky, by Fred K. Schmidt in 1926. It is a variation of a traditional Welsh rarebit.

Make sauce:
Melt butter in a saucepan over medium heat and whisk in flour, stirring until it begins to brown slightly. Whisk in milk slowly to avoid lumps. Bring to a boil, stirring constantly. Mix in white cheddar cheese and hot sauce, and stir in beaten egg to thicken. Remove from the heat and stir in cream.

Preheat the oven's broiler.

Build sandwiches:
Arrange 8 slices of toast on a cookie sheet. Cover each with a liberal amount of roasted turkey and season with salt and pepper. Spoon cheese sauce over top of each sandwich.

Place the cookie sheet under the preheated broiler and cook until speckled brown on top, (about 5 minutes).

Remove and place two slices bacon in a cross shape and tomato slices on top of each sandwich. Sprinkle with Parmigiano-Reggiano cheese.

Dallas, Texas
Cowboy Caviar

Cowboy or Texas Caviar is an easy recipe created by Helen Corbitt, a native New Yorker who became the food service director at Neiman Marcus around 1940 in Dallas, Texas. She first served the dish on New Year's Eve because black-eyed peas are its main ingredient and are said to bring prosperity or good luck according to a Southern tradition. Later, her salad was named "Texas caviar" as a witty comparison to true caviar.

For the dip:
Mix all the Texas caviar dip ingredients in a large mixing bowl, cover, and refrigerate for at least 1 hour or up to 24 hours.

Chill the avocado (whole and unpeeled) for at least one hour. Take off the pit and slice to add to the salad right before serving it to prevent turning brown!

For the dressing:
In another bowl, whisk in all the ingredients for the dressing. Refrigerate covered.

Before serving or about 30 minutes prior, pour the dressing over the Texas caviar and toss until combined. Taste and adjust seasonings if needed.

Serve with corn tortilla chips as a dip, salad, or side dish for meats.

2-15 oz. cans black-eye peas, drained and rinsed
1-15 oz. can black beans, drained and rinsed
1-15 oz. can yellow corn, drained and rinsed
½ Red onion, chopped
1 cup tomatoes, chopped
1 jalapeno, chopped
2 bell peppers, chopped
¼ cup green onions, chopped
1 avocado, chopped
For the dressing:
¼ cup lime juice
¼ cup olive oil
Salt and ground black pepper to taste
2 garlic cloves, minced
½ teaspoon red pepper flakes
½ teaspoon ground cumin
½ teaspoon honey or sugar

New Orleans, Louisiana: Shrimp Po'Boys

Remoulade Sauce
1 cup mayonnaise
2 tablespoons relish
1 tablespoon fresh lemon juice
2 teaspoons hot sauce
2 teaspoons capers, chopped
1½ teaspoons paprika
1 teaspoon Creole mustard
1 teaspoon Worcestershire sauce
2 garlic cloves, minced

For the Fried Shrimp
3 teaspoons kosher salt
2 teaspoons paprika
1 teaspoon garlic powder
½ teaspoon cayenne pepper
½ teaspoon black pepper
2 lbs. raw medium shrimp peeled, deveined, and tail off
Vegetable oil for frying
1½ cup all purpose flour
1 cup cornmeal
1 cup buttermilk
3 tablespoons hot sauce

Po'Boy Sandwich Assembly
4-8 inch long French loaves split
Shredded iceberg lettuce
Sliced tomatoes

In 1929, the "poor boy" was created by Bennie and Clovis Martin, former streetcar conductors that opened Martin Brothers Restaurant in the French Market. When the Streetcars went on strike, they devised a simple but hearty sandwich to give away to the strikers.

When a striking union member walked into their restaurant, Benny would call to Clovis, "Here comes another poor boy!"

For the Remoulade Sauce:
Mix everything together and chill in the refrigerator.

For the Fried Shrimp:
Mix the salt, paprika, garlic powder, cayenne pepper, and black pepper, then divide the spice mixture in half. Season the shrimp with half of the spice mixture. Mix the flour, cornmeal, and the rest of the spice mixture in a bowl.

In a separate bowl, mix the buttermilk and hot sauce. Dip seasoned shrimp in the buttermilk, then coat with flour mixture shaking off any excess. If you like a thicker coating, you can repeat this step. Chill the shrimp in the refrigerator for 20 minutes.

In a cast iron pan, heat the oil to 350°F.
Working in batches, fry shrimp until golden brown, about 3-4 minutes per batch. Transfer to paper towels to drain.

To Assemble Po'Boy
Build your sandwich on French bread with mayonnaise or Remoulade, dress your sandwich with lettuce, tomato, and pickles, then pile on the shrimp.

New York City, New York:
Deli Pastromi Sandwich

2 slices rye bread
½ lb pastrami sliced
½ cup coleslaw
1 slice Swiss cheese
Spicy brown mustard
Kosher dill pickle for garnish

Pastrami on rye is a sandwich that was popularized in the Jewish kosher delicatessens of New York City. It was first created in 1888 by Sussman Volk, who served it at his deli on Delancey Street in New York City.

Pastrami on rye is usually served with the classic accouterments of spicy brown mustard and Kosher dill pickles.

Toast the rye bread on a skillet or grill pan. Set aside.

In a skillet over medium heat, add pastrami and cook until heated through.

Spread mustard evenly on top of one piece of the bread.
Add pastrami and Swiss cheese.

Add coleslaw on top, and then top with another piece of bread.

Cut the sandwiches in half. Serve and enjoy!

GARBAGE PLATE"

Rochester, New York:
The Garbage Plate

Rochester Hot Sauce:

1 lb. 80/20 ground beef

1 cup minced dried onions

1 quart water

1 tablespoon chili powder

1 teaspoon cayenne pepper

1 tablespoon paprika

1 teaspoon cinnamon

Salt to taste

Garbage Plate is a unique mashup of ingredients so widely regarded as Rochester's signature dish that the locals simply call it "plate." This not-for-the-faint-of-heart gastronomic treasure is your choice of cheeseburger, hamburger, Italian sausages, steak, chicken, white or red hots, served on top of any combination of home fries, french fries, baked beans, and/or macaroni salad. The plate is then topped with a spicy Rochester Hot meat sauce, mustard, and onions for added heartburn garnish.

Rochester Hot Sauce is different from your typical hot sauce. The "hot factor" doesn't even reference the spice, but more the actual temperature, as in it is served hot. It's more like a sauce on a chili cheese dog.

Legend has it that Nick Tahou, now celebrating over 100 years in business, invented the plate late one night when some college students entered the restaurant and requested a plate with "all the garbage on it."

In a large pot, brown the ground beef over medium-high heat, using your spoon to break it up. Add the dried onions, water, chili powder, cayenne pepper, paprika, and cinnamon, and stir well.

Bring the pot to a boil and then reduce the heat to medium-low. Simmer for 3 hours, stirring periodically.

Chicago, Illinois: Italian Roast Beef

3 lb. chuck roast, trimmed
1 envelope Italian salad dressing mix
8 oz. pepperoncini pepper slices
¼ cup pepperoncini pepper juice
8 oz. Chicago-style Giardiniera
14.5 oz. can beef broth
Provolone cheese slices
Hoagie buns

The origins are said to lie with Chicago's Italian immigrant population that worked in the stockyards in the early 1900s. When working men would bring home tough meat from the factories that couldn't be sold, they roasted it in spices, sliced it thinly, and served it on rolls to improve the taste. They began serving it at their local weddings and banquets to afford to feed everyone, and the sandwich took off.

Italian Roast Beef is heavily garnished with Chicago-style Giardiniera, a medley of chopped vegetables including cauliflower, carrots, bell peppers, celery, and chile peppers. The veggies are joined together and preserved in a two-step process: First, they're pickled vinegar, and then they're marinated in olive oil.

Place chuck roast into the bottom of a 6-quart crock pot, then sprinkle with salad dressing mix. Add pepperoncini peppers plus a splash of juice, Giardiniera, and beef broth. Place a lid on top then cook on low for 9 hours, or until meat shreds easily with a fork. Shred, then place meat back into crock pot and cook on low for 1 more hour.

Split buns in half then scoop the shredded meat mixture on top and add provolone cheese slices. Top with additional pepperoncini peppers and Giardiniera and serve.

Washington, D.C.:
The Half-Smoke

In Washington, DC, the half-smoke is much more than a sausage. In this town, it's a symbol. They're a combination of ground pork and beef and are smokier and spicier than your standard dog.

At some point, the half-smoke became a fixture on the menu of Ben's Chili Bowl. This restaurant opened in 1958 on DC's U Street, then the central artery of a black neighborhood known for its theaters and jazz clubs. Ben's Chili Bowl is credited with catapulting the half-smoke to local fame. Still, the former movie theater-turned-pool hall-turned-restaurant has become a symbol of longevity and entrepreneurship in the once majority-black "Chocolate City."

Heat up the vegetable oil in a large saucepan or Dutch oven on medium heat and saute the garlic and onion until soft. Add the ground beef to the mix and saute until the meat is browned. Add the remaining ingredients once the meat is browned, and turn the heat low. Cover the chili and let simmer for at least 40 minutes, stirring occasionally.

On a grill, heat the sausages, turning them frequently to char them all over.

Split a half-smoke on a bun, smother it in the chili, and add a couple of pinches of cheese.

4 Half-Smokes
1 tablespoon vegetable oil
1 large onion, chopped
1 garlic clove, minced
3 tablespoons chili powder
1 tablespoon sugar
1 teaspoon cumin
1 teaspoon cinnamon
1 teaspoon curry powder
¼ teaspoon cayenne pepper
1 lbs. ground beef
2½ tablespoons tomato paste
3 tablespoons corn meal
3 teaspoons salt
1 teaspoon pepper
2 cups chicken stock
1 bay Leaf
4 hotdog rolls
¼ Cup Cheddar Cheese, shredded

Milwaukee, Wisconsin: Fried Cheese Curds

2 quarts corn oil for frying
1 cup all-purpose flour
¾ cup beer
¼ cup milk
2 eggs
½ teaspoon salt
2 pounds cheese curds

Cheese curds, a uniquely Wisconsin delicacy, are formed as a by-product of the cheese-making process. Virtually every restaurant, bar, and bowling alley in Wisconsin seems to serve them. Most Wisconsin cheese curd is a cheddar cheese product, but some can be made from mozzarella, Colby, or Monterey Jack cheeses.

Wisconsinites are so addicted to their fromage that they lovingly refer to themselves as "cheeseheads" and even wear funky Styrofoam cheese hats at Green Bay Packers football games.

Heat corn oil in a deep-fryer or large saucepan to 375°F.

Whisk together flour, beer, milk, eggs, and salt to form a smooth, thin batter.

Place cheese curds, about 6 or 8 at a time, into the batter, stir to coat and remove with a wire strainer. Shake the curds to remove excess batter.

Deep fry curds in hot oil until golden brown, 1 or 2 minutes. Drain on paper towels; serve hot.

Lancaster, Pennsylvania
Scrapple

5 pounds boneless pork butt
1 large onion, quartered
1 whole bulb garlic, sliced in half
4 bay leaves
1 tablespoon black peppercorns
1 stalk celery
2 teaspoons salt

Spice Mix:

1 tablespoon black pepper
1 tablespoon salt
1 tablespoon savory
2 teaspoons poultry seasoning
1 teaspoon dried thyme
1 teaspoon ground white pepper
½ teaspoon cayenne

To Finish:

2 heaping cups cornmeal
½ cup buckwheat flour

Mystery meat. Scrapple, a traditional Pennsylvania Dutch food, is typically made with pork scraps or parts you might otherwise discard, such as trotters (feet), liver, heart, and the parts that go over the fence last. Some recipes even use the head of the animal. This version uses pork butt.

Place the pork in a large stockpot or Dutch oven along with the quartered onion, garlic bulb, bay leaves, peppercorns, and 2 teaspoons of salt. Cover with water (at least 5 to 6 cups) and boil over high heat. Reduce the heat to low and simmer for 3 hours.

Remove the pork pieces to a bowl, set them aside, strain the broth into a bowl, and discard the solids. When the pork is cool enough to handle, shred it and remove any bones. Measure 4 cups of the pork broth into a large saucepan and add the sage, thyme, and oregano. Bring the broth to a boil; reduce the heat to low, and simmer for 5 minutes.

Strain your pork broth and pour about 4 cups into a large pot. Bring this to a simmer and add the cornmeal and buckwheat flour, stirring often, about 30 minutes. Add the shredded pork in with the mush and stir well to combine.Let this all cook for 10 minutes or so.

Pour this into loaf pans, or a terrine pan. Pack it in well. Let it cool to room temperature uncovered, then cover it with plastic wrap and refrigerate overnight until firm.

Fry Scrapple
Heat 2 tablespoons of vegetable oil in a heavy skillet. Cut the scrapple into ¾-inch slices and fry the slices for about 3 to 4 minutes on each side, or until crisp and golden brown.

St. Louis: Missouri: Toasted Ravioli

2 tablespoons whole milk

1 egg

¾ cup Italian seasoned bread crumbs

½ teaspoon salt

1 (12 oz.) package frozen cheese ravioli, thawed

3 cups vegetable oil for frying

1 tablespoon grated Parmesan cheese

1 (16 oz.) jar spaghetti sauce

Toasted ravioli, colloquially known as T-Ravs, is breaded deep-fried ravioli, usually served as an appetizer but can also be used to consume dipping sauce. It was created and popularized in St. Louis, Missouri at two restaurants, Mama Campisi's and Charlie Gitto's.

Combine milk and egg in a small bowl. Place breadcrumbs and if desired, salt in a shallow bowl. Dip ravioli in milk mixture, and coat with breadcrumbs.

In a large saucepan, heat marinara sauce over medium heat until bubbling. Reduce the heat to simmer.

In a large, heavy pan, pour oil to a depth of 2 inches. Heat oil over medium heat until a small amount of breading sizzles and turns brown. Fry ravioli, a few at a time, 1 minute on each side or until golden. Drain on paper towels. Sprinkle with Parmesan cheese and serve immediately with hot marinara sauce.

New Orleans, Louisiana:
Gumbo

For the Roux:

1 heaping cup all-purpose flour
2/3 cup canola oil

For the Gumbo:

8 cups chicken broth
1 bunch celery, diced
1 green bell pepper, diced
1 large yellow onion, diced
1 bunch green onion, finely chopped
1 bunch parsley, finely chopped
3 cloves garlic
2 teaspoons dried thyme
2 bay leaves
½ teaspoon cayenne pepper
2 tablespoons Cajun seasoning
12 ounce andouille sausages or Polska Kielbasa
2 cups Shrimp
Cooked white rice for serving

Gumbo is Louisiana's love language. This humble southern stew represents the marriage of cultures, subtleties of tradition, local ingredients, and, above all, community. For many families in South Louisiana, gumbo is a weekly ritual.

In a large, heavy-bottom stock pot, combine flour and oil. Cook on medium-low heat, stirring constantly for 30-45 minutes. When it's finished, it should be as dark as chocolate and have the consistency of soft cookie dough. You can add more flour or oil as needed to reach this consistency. Be careful not to let it burn!

In a separate skillet on medium-high heat, brown the sausage. Remove to a plate. Add ½ cup of the chicken broth to the hot sausage skillet to deglaze the pan. Pour the broth and drippings into a large soup pot.

Add remaining chicken broth, vegetables, parsley, garlic, dry spices, and roux to the pot and stir well.

Bring to a boil over medium heat until the vegetables are slightly tender. Skim off any foam that may rise to the top of the pot. Stir in cajun seasoning to taste, and add chicken, sausage, and shrimp.

Serve warm over rice.

Boston, Massachusetts: Clam Chowder

4 bacon strips, center-cut
2 celery ribs, chopped
1 large onion, chopped
1 garlic clove, minced
3 small potatoes, cubed
1 bottle (8 oz.) clam juice
¼ teaspoon salt
1 cup chicken broth
2 chicken bouillon cubes
¼ teaspoon white pepper
¼ teaspoon dried thyme
⅓ cup all-purpose flour
2 cups half-and-half, divided
2 tablespoons butter
¾ cup fresh clams, chopped, or 2 cans (6.5 oz. each) chopped clams, undrained
Fresh parsley for serving

Food historians believe that New England clam chowder, occasionally called "Boston Clam Chowder," was introduced by French or Nova Scotian settlers. It is made with clams and potatoes with a milk or cream base. It is usually thick and hearty; however, it was quite thin in the 19th and 20th centuries. Boston's Union Oyster House – the oldest continuously operating restaurant in the United States has been serving it since 1836.

While the New England variety is the best known, there are many other variations of clam chowder. New Yorkers insist on tomatoes in their chowder and call it this heinous bilge Manhattan clam chowder. Cookbook writer and chef James Beard described Manhattan clam chowder as: "that rather horrendous soup called Manhattan clam chowder. . . resembles a vegetable soup that accidentally had some clams dumped into it."

In a Dutch oven, cook bacon over medium heat until crisp. Remove to paper towels to drain; set aside. Saute celery and onion in the drippings until tender. Add garlic; cook 1 minute longer. Stir in the potatoes, clam juice, chicken broth, bouillon cubes, salt, pepper, and thyme. Bring to a boil. Reduce heat; simmer, uncovered, until potatoes are tender, 15-20 minutes.

In a small bowl, combine flour, butter, and 1 cup half-and-half until smooth. Gradually stir into soup. Bring to a boil; cook and stir until thickened, 1-2 minutes.

Stir in clams and remaining half-and-half and heat through (do not boil). Crumble the cooked bacon and sprinkle over each serving. Garnish with parsley.

Columbus, Ohio: Shredded Chicken Sandwich

1½ lbs. boneless skinless chicken breasts

1 can condensed cream of chicken soup

6 ounces chicken flavored stuffing mix

Chicken broth (for thinning if the mixture seems to thick)

Coleslaw for garnish

Hamburger buns

Invented as a way to use leftover chicken, these sandwiches became popular for covered dish dinners, potlucks, church dinners, and tailgate parties. They are also sold in small-town Ohio restaurants, drive-ins, and bars.

While it's economical and easy to make, the signature combination of ingredients makes it so classic.

Place the chicken breasts in the slow cooker. Pour the condensed soup overtop. Cover and cook on low for 3-4 hours or until the chicken is shreddable.

Shred the chicken, then add the stuffing mix. Mix well, cover, and cook for 15-20 minutes or until the bread crumbs are moistened.

To make the mixture thinner, add a little chicken broth until it is the desired consistency.

Garnish with Coleslaw. Serve on hamburger buns.

Ithaca, New York: Cornell Chicken

- 4-bone-in, split chicken breasts with skin on
- ½ cup vegetable oil
- 1 cup apple cider vinegar
- 4 cloves garlic, crushed
- 4 tablespoons Worcestershire Sauce
- 2 teaspoons poultry seasoning
- 2 tablespoon sugar
- 1½ teaspoon celery salt
- 1½ teaspoon salt
- ½ teaspoon white pepper
- ½ teaspoon black pepper

Cornell University poultry scientist Dr. Robert C. Baker created Cornell Chicken. He was trying to invent an easy and delicious way to grill smaller, younger chickens to help the local chicken farms sell more birds.

In Upstate New York, you'll find this deliciously cooked bird served at benefit events, community auctions, church functions, family reunions, and in and around just about any life event that can be accompanied by food. Cornell Chicken is the unofficial food of the New York State Fair, which goes through 40,000 chickens every year.

In a medium mixing bowl, combine all ingredients except chicken.

Pierce chicken with a fork several times to allow marinade to really sink in. Place chicken quarters into a large airtight plastic bag or other tight fitting container. Cover with marinade, reserving a ½ cup for basting. Refrigerate for 2 - 24 hours.

Heat grill to medium-high heat. You can use either gas or long burning charcoal. Place chicken on the grill on indirect heat.

Use reserved marinade, basting the chicken throughout the cooking process. Cook over indirect heat for 30-35 minutes, turning and basting.

At 35 minutes, transfer to direct heat to get a crispy and good char marks. Remove from the grill and allow to rest for 5-10 minutes before serving. Discard any unused marinade.

Buffalo, New York:
Beef on Weck

A Beef on Weck is a sandwich made with roast beef on a Kummelweck roll, a roll that is topped with kosher salt and caraway seeds. Predating the chicken wing by over a century, legend has it that in the 1800s an immigrant from the Black Forest had a bar on the waterfront in Buffalo. He wanted to feed his hungry drinking customers, so he thought putting roast beef on a roll that he remembered from the old world, which was topped with coarse salt and caraway seed, would encourage his patrons to purchase more drinks.

In a bowl, add water to yeast and mix to activate. Add honey, oil, and half of the flour and mix until combined. Add salt and the remaining flour. Mix on low speed until combined, and then increase speed slightly and mix for 5 to 8 minutes. Place dough in an oiled bowl, cover, and let rise in a warm spot for 1 hour. After 1 hour, punch down the dough and let rise again for another 30 minutes.

After the second rise, cut the dough into 6 pieces and shape into a ball. Place rolls on acornmeal dusted baking sheet and let rise in a warm place for 30 minutes or until doubled.

Preheat oven to 425°F.
Prepare a baking sheet by lining with parchment paper and lightly sprinkling it with cornmeal. Before putting the bread in the oven, spray the oven very well with water and then spray the rolls with water just before loading and after 2, and 5 minutes of baking.

Brush the top of proofed rolls with egg white, and sprinkle them with kosher salt and caraway seeds. Bake until lightly browned-about 10-15 minutes.

Dip 4 oz. portions of sliced roast beef in au jus until meat is warmed through. Place dipped beef on the bottom of a sliced Kummelweck roll. Add a dollop of fresh horseradish.

Dough: *(6 rolls)*
2 teaspoons instant dry yeast
1 cup warm water
2 tablespoons vegetable oil
1 egg white
1½ tablespoons sugar
2 teaspoons table salt
1 teaspoon honey
3-3½ cups bread flour

For Baking:
1 egg white
Kosher salt
Caraway seeds
Cornmeal to line baking sheet

For Sandwich:
32 oz. beef au jus
Horseradish

Maine:
Spudnut/ Yankee Potato Doughnut

2 -¼ oz. packages active dry yeast
½ cup warm water
½ cup hot mashed potatoes
1 ½ cup scalded milk
½ cup canola oil
½ cup sugar
2 eggs , beaten
1 teaspoon salt
7½ cups all-purpose flour
Additional oil for deep-fat frying
4 cups confectioners' sugar
⅓ cup water
1 teaspoon vanilla extract

In 1937, Yankee magazine published a recipe for "Maine Potato Doughnuts." Yankee Potato Doughnuts, sometimes called a Spudnut, are fluffy, soft, tender, and moist. Although they're prepared in a similar way, doughnuts made with mashed potatoes tend to be lighter than their all-flour doughnut cousins.

In the 18th century, German immigrants in Pennsylvania deep fried potato-based doughnuts the day before Ash Wednesday to help eliminate sugar and fat sitting around the house.

The first doughnut chain in the United States was not Krispy Kreme or Dunkin Donuts, but a Utah-based franchise named Spudnuts. In the 1940s and '50s, the owners took potato-based doughnuts mainstream, opening hundreds of stores. The originating company eventually declared bankruptcy, but a few independent stores remain.

In a large bowl, dissolve yeast in warm water. Add the mashed potatoes, milk, oil, sugar, eggs, and salt. Add enough flour to form a soft dough.

Place in a greased bowl, turning once to grease top. Cover and let rise in a warm place until doubled, about 1 hour. Punch dough down; let rise again until doubled, about 20 minutes.

Roll out on a floured surface to ½ -inch thickness. Cut with a floured 3-inch doughnut cutter.

In a cast iron skillet, heat oil to 375°F. Fry doughnuts, a few at a time, until golden brown.

For glaze, in a large bowl, combine the confectioners' sugar, water, and vanilla until smooth. Dip warm doughnuts in glaze.

Cool on wire racks. Consider Weight Watchers.

About the Author

In addition to being a slightly off-bubble cook who likes to chase his wife around the kitchen, Dr. Maddog, aka Mark Donnelly, PhD. is an artist, educator, community activist, Freemason, and a proud husband, father, and grandfather.

Dr. Donnelly has written several cookbooks, including *50 Shades of Gravy, Goose the Cook, Survival Juice, Poultry in Motion, and How to Eat a Buffalo.* He is also author of a series of children's books and books about his hometown Buffalo, New York.

www.ingramcontent.com/pod-product-compliance
Lightning Source LLC
LaVergne TN
LVHW060640110826
845147LV00018B/1017

* 9 7 8 1 9 5 6 6 8 8 1 5 3 *